*In honour of our precious baby*

## ABOUT THE AUTHOR

Shaela Mauger and Harpermartin

Born and raised in Wagga Wagga regional New South Wales, Shaela has pursued her love of graphic design through university and began her career as a designer for a local printer.

Since becoming a mother, Shaela has fine tuned her passion for design towards what's most important to her: loved ones, and cherishing the time we have with them. Now, after half a decade of having her own design business, Shaela has launched Harpermartin — paying homage to her parents' family names — and this series of keepsake books, created to celebrate life and love in all its forms.

The series is available at www.harpermartin.com.au

Copyright © Shaela Mauger 2019
Original cover painting © Fay Mifsud 2019

All rights reserved. No part of this publication may be reproduced, stored in a retrieval system or transmitted, in any form or by any means, electronic, mechanical, photocopying, recording or otherwise, without prior permission of the copyright holder.

ISBN 978-0-6482778-3-5

Designed in collaboration with
The Pink Elephants Support Network

# Remembering Me
EARLY PREGNANCY LOSS EDITION

By Shaela Mauger

Cover watercolour painting by Faenerys
www.faenerys.com

**ACKNOWLEDGEMENTS;**

This book would not be possible without the help and support of many beautiful people.

Firstly Samantha and Gabbi of the Pink Elephants Support Network, for collaborating with me to create this beautiful book.

Secondly Rachel Bridge, Laura Smothers-Chu, Pam Wakefield, Ann-Marie Imrie, Terry Diamond, Samantha Payne and Gabriel Soh for allowing me to share their stories.

Finally to every single person that completed my survey, answered my questions on social media or provided input, your support has been invaluable and by sharing your journey you have allowed me to help others in their journey through early pregnancy loss.

# TABLE OF CONTENTS

| | |
|---|---|
| Preface | 1 |
| Recognition Of Pregnancy | 3 |
| Our First Ultrasound | 3 |
| The Day Your Heart Stopped Beating | 3 |
| Diary | 7-15 |
| Dads Grieve Too... | 17-23 |
| Dreams Of Who You Could Have Been... | 25-27 |
| Marking The Loss | 29-53 |

**FOR HELP AND SUPPORT ;**

**Pink Elephants Support Network** - pinkelephantssupport.com

**Bears Of Hope** - bearsofhope.org.au

**Sands** - sands.org.au

*"For a mother...it is a loss in every sense of the word. Physical, tangible, emotional, relational. Third time around when we fell pregnant, our minds and our hearts went straight to the little person who was joining our family."*

RACHEL BRIDGE
@ rachelbridge_mamabefrank

## PREFACE

Every baby deserves to be honoured and cherished. With the help of The Pink Elephants Support Network, this book was designed to provide comfort and support during the devastating journey of early pregnancy loss. It includes space to put your grief into words and mark your loss in a very thoughtful, beautiful way.

Although your baby may not be here with you on Earth today, they will forever hold a place in your heart.

With love,

*Shaela* xx

Founder, Harpermartin

"No words can describe losing a heartbeat, especially when you've seen it fluttering quickly below your own. It is difficult to describe the physical and emotional feelings of labour pain, especially the agony you have to endure without a crying baby to reward you at the end."

LAURA SMOTHERS-CHU
CEO & Founder of Befriended Heart

## RECOGNITION OF PREGNANCY

On this day, _____ we found out we were going to be parents.

Our reaction was: _____

_____

_____

## OUR FIRST ULTRASOUND

## THE DAY YOUR HEART STOPPED BEATING

On this day, _____ at _____ weeks we were given the devastating news that your heart was no longer beating.

# Its ok

## REMEMBER

It's **OK** to feel completely devastated.

It's **OK** to hide away from well-meaning family and friends and give yourself space to process and grieve your loss. You have not only lost a baby, but also all the hopes and dreams that you had for them.

It's **OK** to be jealous of anyone who has a baby or announces a new pregnancy.

It's **OK** to have days where you cry, even a few months after the miscarriage.

It's **OK** to feel temporarily disconnected from your other children.

It's **OK** to grieve differently to your partner.

It's **OK** to get ridiculously angry for no reason at all.

It's **OK** to feel like you need to control every other aspect of your life.

It's **OK** to question why this happened to you.

It's **OK** to lose your confidence in other areas of your life.

It's **OK** to feel like a failure as a woman.

It's **OK** to believe that you will never have a baby.

It's **OK** to be obsessed with conceiving another baby.

It's **OK** to never want to try and have another baby.

It's **OK** to want to obsessively hold and cuddle other people's babies.

It's **OK** to not want to even look at anyone else's baby.

It's **OK** to want someone to guarantee that it will never happen again.

It's **OK** to feel completely out of control when no-one can do this.

It's **OK** to feel none of the above and move on from the experience with little effect on your life.

*Contributed by Terry Diamond - Perinatal Bereavement Counsellor*

*"You might want to write and that's great because journaling is a great way to get thoughts out of your head. No one else has to see what you've written unless you want them to, so see if you can allow yourself to write whatever comes up without censoring yourself."*

                    PAM WAKEFIELD AThR
                    Registered Arts Therapist
          Beyond the Silence - arts therapy for pregnancy loss

# DIARY

"You're not alone. There are a lot of us dads. Allow yourself to feel what you're feeling for as long as you're feeling it. It's ok too if you're not feeling anything. But if you're hurting, or in pain, find a way to release it. Writing helped me. Connecting with other dads of loss helped me. Music helped me".

GABRIEL SOH
lovecommadad.com

## DADS GRIEVE TOO...

You are allowed to be upset and have time to grieve. Feeling emotional or sad about losing your baby does not make you any less of a man. There is nothing either of you did for this to happen and hopefully, in time, your partner will be pregnant again with a healthy baby.

Seek out someone you know that may have also gone through something similar and have a chat to them about it. One in six pregnancies end before twenty weeks, this is not to diminish your feelings of grief, but to let you know that you are not alone.

If you or your partner are still not coping after a few weeks, please speak to your GP and seek medical advice/counselling.

The next few pages are for you to write down your thoughts and feelings. A place to put your grief into words if and when you choose.

"With our first miscarriage, I didn't have any immediate feelings. My concern went directly to my wife. How was she feeling? Was she okay? I tried to remain as calm as possible for her and for our son.

Thinking back, to all our miscarriages, my immediate response was to comfort my wife. It wasn't until a day or so afterwards that I started to address my own feelings. I felt sad. I felt an emptiness. I felt lost. I had already been planning what our future would be like with our newborn. I put away the names I'd picked out. A list of girl's names. A list of boy's names. My feelings of loss, of grief, of mourning, were generally put aside".

GABRIEL SOH
lovecommadad.com

## WHAT CAN YOU DO FOR YOUR PARTNER

She needs you more than ever during this time. Don't try to fix it just let her talk. We know that you just want to make everything better, remember though, having a miscarriage is one of the most painful events a woman can experience. Patience, love and understanding are key in helping her recover and feel like herself again.

BE THERE
If you can take a day or two off work on the day of D&C (dilatation and curettage - performed in an operating theatre under a general anaesthetic to remove remaining pregnancy tissue) or physical miscarriage, do so. Look at cancelling any pre-organised plans and just be there for her.

BE UNDERSTANDING
She needs acknowledgement of her loss and to validate her grief. Remember the baby was growing inside her body and her body has gone through many changes. She may feel empty and desperately wishing to feel and still be pregnant.

BE PATIENT
Try not to pressure her to 'get over it'. Give her the time she needs. She is on a rollercoaster of tears, anger, confusion and hurt. She may snap at you, she doesn't mean to, it is just her grief overwhelming her.

BE GUIDED BY HER
Be guided by her. Some women may cry, some may not. Some may want to talk, others may not. Grief is a very personal experience and she needs you to just 'be there' as she goes through it.

TELL HER THAT YOU LOVE HER
She really needs to hear this from you. She may have terrible feelings of guilt that her body has failed her and she has let you down in some way. She needs to know that you are going to get through this together and this is no-one's fault.

TALKING TO OTHERS
It can be really helpful for her to speak to someone that has been through the same thing; a friend, or support group. If she feels she needs it, encourage her to seek professional help.

*Extracted from the The Pink Elephants Support Network 'Partner Advice' brochure.*

DREAMS OF WHO YOU COULD HAVE BEEN...

*"You could have been an astronaut, up among the stars and you would have been a pioneer — the first to go to Mars"...*

ANN-MAREE IMRIE

anniemauthor.com
Author 'You Could Have Been...'

*In memory of Xavier Rocket Imrie*

# DREAMS OF WHO YOU COULD HAVE BEEN...

## MARKING THE LOSS

Everybody grieves differently. Everyones journey is different, but remembering your baby and doing something special to mark the loss can often be helpful and healing in your time of grieving.

The next section of this book provides a platform to mark certain stages and days throughout the grieving process. It is aided by headings but is essentially a blank canvas for you to fill in however you wish. It provides a way to put your grief into words and mark the loss of your precious baby.

Other ideas to mark the loss include:

- Holding a Ceremony
- Lighting a candle in memory of your baby
- Plant a tree or purchase a statue or water feature
- Create a small shrine to honour your baby's memory

*Extracted from the The Pink Elephants Support Network 'Marking the Loss' brochure.*

"First trimester loss is complicated. You see for everyone, typically outside of the family unit, there is no loss, no sign, no indication, no representation of tangible loss. There are even statistics that suggest that loss is expected, normal, ok....insignificant??
For the family, there is the loss of what should have been.... We lost the baby that we had already made space for in our minds, in our hearts and in our family.  We lost the baby we had begun planning and prepping for...where will he or she sleep, how old will his or her sisters and brother be...when will he or she be here to meet us..."

RACHEL BRIDGE
@ rachelbridge_mamabefrank

TODAY I WOULD BE _____ WEEKS PREGNANT

*a love letter to you*

TODAY I WOULD BE _____ WEEKS PREGNANT

*a love letter to you*

"When experiencing first trimester loss, how do you seek the support, the time, the condolences you need for a loss that to others, is unknown, insignificant, intangible?

My answer is...frankly.... I don't know, and the reason for that is...it's your journey. Listen to yourself, and say 'ok'. If you need support, seek it. If you need space, seek it. If you need time to grieve, take it. If you need to dive back into normal, do it. But whatever you do, treat yourself kindly as you go. Let go of the should."

RACHEL BRIDGE
@ rachelbridge_mamabefrank

TODAY I WOULD BE _____ WEEKS PREGNANT

TODAY I WOULD BE _____ WEEKS PREGNANT

*a love letter to you*

*"A heart full of shoulds and what ifs, a head full of questions, a heart full of longing and yearning for the babies I'd lost and the future children I wanted."*

SAMANTHA PAYNE

Co-Founder The Pink Elephants Support Network

# TODAY, WOULD HAVE BEEN YOUR

_a love letter to you_

# TODAY, WOULD HAVE BEEN YOUR

*a love letter to you*

"Be kind to yourself and don't let other people make you feel worse than you are already feeling. If I have learnt anything as a baby loss mum and a therapist working with families that have lost their babies, it is that 'this too shall pass'. It does get easier with time and you do build a strength and resilience to deal with distress that you could never have imagined was possible. Most people don't get over it, they get through it and the intensity of your pain will fade as time goes on no matter where your journey takes you."

TERRY DIAMOND
Perinatal Bereavement Counsellor

# TODAY, WOULD HAVE BEEN YOUR

*a love letter to you*

*"Miscarriage may be an individual journey, but no woman should have to walk it alone."*

SAMANTHA PAYNE & GABBI ARMSTRONG
Founders The Pink Elephants Support Network

This book was designed with the support of
The Pink Elephants Support Network

pinkelephantssupport.com
support@pinkelephantssupport.com

Big hugs from
www.harpermartin.com.au